LITTLE LOUIS AND THE JAZZ BAND

ALSO BY ANGELA SHELF MEDEARIS

Dare to Dream
Coretta Scott King and the Civil Rights Movement

Annie's Gifts
Come This Far to Freedom
Dancing with the Indians
Our People
Picking Peas for a Penny
The Zebra-Riding Cowboy

LITTLE LOUIS
AND THE
JAZZ BAND

The Story of Louis "Satchmo" Armstrong

by ANGELA SHELF MEDEARIS
illustrated by ANNA RICH

A RAINBOW BIOGRAPHY

LODESTAR BOOKS
Dutton   New York

Text copyright © 1994 by Angela Shelf Medearis

Illustrations copyright © 1994 by Anna Rich

Photographs in this book are from the Jack Bradley Collection, courtesy of Jack Bradley.

Library of Congress Cataloging-in-Publication Data

Medearis, Angela Shelf, 1956–
    Little Louis and the jazz band: the story of Louis "Satchmo" Armstrong / by Angela Shelf Medearis; illustrated by Anna Rich— 1st ed.
        p.   cm.—(A Rainbow biography)
    Includes bibliographical references and index.
    ISBN 0-525-67424-1
    1. Armstrong, Louis, 1900–1971—Juvenile literature. 2. Jazz musicians—United States—Biography—Juvenile literature. [1. Armstrong, Louis, 1900–1971. 2. Musicians. 3. Afro-Americans— Biography.]   I. Rich, Anna, 1956–   ill.   II. Title.   III. Series.
ML3930.A75M5   1994
781.65'092—dc20
[B]
                                                            93-23596
                                                               CIP
                                                            AC MN

Published in the United States by Lodestar Books, an affiliate of Dutton Children's Books, a division of Penguin Books USA Inc., 375 Hudson Street, New York, New York 10014

Published simultaneously in Canada by McClelland & Stewart, Toronto

Editor: Rosemary Brosnan
Designer: Richard Granald, LMD

Printed in the U.S.A.   First Edition
10 9 8 7 6 5 4 3 2 1

CONTENTS

1 BACK O' TOWN

Down South in New Orleans, Louisiana, there lived a boy whom the children called "Dippermouth" because of his wide smile. All the adults called him "Little Louis." His real name was Louis Armstrong, and he was born on August 4, 1901. He lived with his mother, Mary Albert, whom he called Mayann, and his younger sister, Beatrice, whom he called Mama Lucy. His father, William Armstrong, seldom visited Little Louis or his sister.

Little Louis grew up in a poor but lively section of New Orleans called Back o' Town. Every morning he woke up to the melodious cries of the street vendors who strolled through Back o' Town. Singing could be heard throughout the day. The stevedores on the waterfront bellowed out rhythmic work chants as they unloaded the ships. The washerwomen sang mournful spirituals as they scrubbed their loads of clothes. Day and night, tinkly

1

ragtime music danced out of the neighborhood honky-tonks.

Most of the ragtime songs were written by Scott Joplin, a famous black composer. He was called the "King of the Ragtime Writers" because of all the wonderful music he composed. The honky-tonk players on Liberty and Perdido Streets thumped out his ragtime songs in $\frac{2}{4}$ time on the worn keys of upright pianos.

At night, Little Louis fell asleep to the sad songs of the local blues singers. Those sorrowful songs sounded like they were full of all the pain in the world. Sometimes the soft, sweet strains of violin music played by the Creole orchestras for the white folks' parties drifted down to Back o' Town.

Little Louis enjoyed all kinds of music. But he loved the music the brass bands played most of all. Almost every week a brass band performed in a parade somewhere in New Orleans. Most of the parades were put on by one of the black social aid and pleasure clubs like the Zulus, the Tammanys, and the Autocrats.

The club leader always rode at the head of the parade on a beautiful horse with ribbons in its mane. A booming brass band followed behind, playing a merry march. The high-stepping, sharply dressed club members pranced down the street to the band's ringing beat. The club members looked so fine in their white felt hats and their white uniforms! Colorful silk ribbons streamed down from their shoulders. The *rum-tum-tum* of the big bass drum made the crowd on the sidewalk fall in line and step in time. Little Louis followed those parades all over New Orleans.

Special band music was also performed during church and funeral services. After the service, processions of black-clad mourners would tuck parasols under their arms. Then they would walk slowly to the graveyard as a brass band solemnly played "Nearer My God to Thee." The measured, muffled sounds of the snare drum and the sobbing wail of the cornet often brought tears to Little Louis's eyes.

After the funeral was over, the band would slowly lead the mourners out of the graveyard. Then, like the sun coming out from behind a dark cloud, the band would play happy notes, full of jubilation, to celebrate life and the sweetness of living. Beating his snare drum quickly, the drummer would tap out a snazzy riff, *tum-tum a tum, tum-tum a tum.* The cornet player would blast a series of ringing golden notes into the air. *Da-da day da, da-da day da!* Then the band would slide into songs like "When the Saints Go Marching In" and "Didn't He Ramble."

The wild beat of the music sent electric chills through Little Louis from his head down to his feet. Soon the sad expressions on the mourners' faces changed to smiles. They opened their parasols, which were decorated with satin ribbons and

strips of bright crepe paper. As the mourners twirled the parasol handles the multicolored ribbons and crepe paper whipped around and around.

The band's magical music moved Little Louis so much that before he knew what he was doing he'd join the second line of people who followed the mourners. Little Louis clapped his hands and swayed with the crowd from one side of the street to the other.

Sometimes after a parade, Joe "King" Oliver, the best cornet player in New Orleans, would let Little Louis carry his cornet case. That made Little Louis feel like a king himself!

Little Louis wanted to make music too. He wanted to play a cornet just like King Oliver!

2 THE COLORED WAIFS' HOME FOR BOYS

Ever since he was seven years old, Little Louis had worked after school to help his mother. He sold buckets of coal late into the night. During that time, people used coal for heating and for cooking. Little Louis blew a tin party horn so that everyone would know he had coal to sell. He found that if he took the wooden mouthpiece off the horn and used two fingers over the end of the mouthpiece hole, he could play a tune. He wanted a real trumpet, but he was too poor to buy one. All the money he earned went to help Mayann.

Every night Little Louis and his friends would stand on a street corner and blow harmonicas and scrape the tops of tin cans together to draw a crowd. One of Louis's friends would balance upside down on his head on top of a bean can. Then he would spin around and around and around. Whenever a crowd gathered, the group would break into "My Brazilian Beauty," in a mellow four-part harmony. Little Louis sang tenor. Then someone would pass a hat around to collect tips from the audience.

Close to midnight, on December 31, 1912, Little Louis quietly slipped out of his house and ran down the street. The fear of being caught made him move swiftly. He had a gun he'd taken from its hiding place at home. Little Louis and his friends thought it would be fun to shoot off some blanks once the New Year began. And that's just what he did. When the clock began to chime, Little Louis fired his gun with a loud bang six times.

Before he knew what was happening, a policeman had grabbed Little Louis by the arm. "Please, mister, don't arrest me," begged Little Louis. "I won't do it no more! Please, let me go back to Mama. I won't do it no more."[1] It was no use. Off Little Louis went, in the custody of the New Orleans police.

The judge decided to send Little Louis to the Colored Waifs' Home for Boys to keep him out of trouble. Captain Joseph Jones and his wife ran the Home, which was out in the country near a dairy farm. The Home gave poor children who were in trouble with the law a chance to finish school and learn a trade like carpentry or gardening.

Captain Jones was a military man. He ran the Home army-style. A bugler woke up the boys each morning. They had a certain amount of time to

dress, eat, and finish their chores. The boys drilled with wooden guns. Then they attended school.

Little Louis was heartbroken and homesick. For days he could barely eat. He was quickly punished whenever he broke a rule. Then one day, Little Louis heard something that made him smile. He began to clap his hands and tap his feet. A brass band was playing!

Little Louis followed the sound of the music.

Soon he found himself in a room full of boys with instruments. There were all kinds of instruments—drums, trombones, clarinets, tubas, French horns, and cornets! Little Louis wanted to play in the band. He attended band rehearsals day after day, waiting patiently for a chance to play.

3 LEADER OF THE BAND

One day, Peter Davis, the conductor of the band, said, "Louis Armstrong, how would you like to join our brass band?"[2] Louis was so surprised he couldn't speak. Mr. Davis asked him again.

"I certainly would, Mr. Davis," said Louis happily. "I certainly would!" He could see himself all decked out in the snappy band uniform with his eyes closed, blowing a cornet.

The first instrument Mr. Davis gave Little Louis was a tambourine. Little Louis beat the tambourine in perfect time.

Then Mr. Davis told Little Louis to try the drums. The band began to play "At the Animals' Ball." During a break in the song, Little Louis pounded out a brassy beat. Mr. Davis smiled and tapped his feet. All the boys shouted, "Hooray for Louis Armstrong!"

Next, Mr. Davis gave Little Louis the alto saxophone to play, and finally a cornet. Happy day!

Mr. Davis helped Little Louis learn how to play his cornet properly. He showed Little Louis how to hold his mouth and use his breathing, his throat, and his stomach muscles to produce a good tone. He also made him the Home's bugler. Little Louis woke the boys each morning with the rousing song "I Can't Get 'Em Up." He lulled them to sleep at night with "Taps."

Little Louis soon mastered all of the songs the band played. He became so good on the cornet that Mr. Davis made him leader of the band!

Little Louis felt honored to wear the bandleader's special outfit. He put on the cream-colored pants, brown stockings, brown tennis shoes, and cream-colored cap. The other band members wore blue and black uniforms. The boys often paraded all around New Orleans. Little Louis was proud when the band marched through his neighborhood. His mother and sister watched as Little Louis led the band in their songs. After their performance, his neighbors passed the hat. There was enough money for new instruments and uniforms!

Little Louis loved playing his cornet. Sometimes he played soft, sweet harmonies. Sometimes his cornet shook the walls with the spirited tunes Little Louis had heard King Oliver play. And sometimes Little Louis played unwritten music from deep down in his heart.

In 1914, when Louis was thirteen years old, he was allowed to leave the Colored Waifs' Home. He was sorry to say good-bye to Captain Jones, Mr. Davis, and all the boys. But he was happy to see his mother and Mama Lucy again.

Louis Armstrong wasn't "little" anymore. He'd grown from a small boy into a young man determined to make it in life. After two years of hard work, he had become a talented musician. Louis felt that he was finally ready to play with musicians like King Oliver and bandleader Kid Ory. He was determined to be the best cornet player in New Orleans.

4 JAZZ!

Louis noticed that something had changed while he was in the Colored Waifs' Home. New Orleans music was different. Ragtime music was almost gone. A swinging new type of music was being played. Some people called this kind of music "jazz."

Playing jazz was quite a feat. Instead of the old $\frac{2}{4}$ time, it had a red-hot $\frac{4}{4}$ beat. There was a constant *boom-chicka-boom, boom-chicka-boom* rhythm in the jazz songs. Jazz music was like the sausage, crab, and shrimp jambalaya, mixed with the rich red beans and rice, that Louis's mother made. It was a spicy mix of African drum rhythms, work songs that slaves had sung, and gospel hymns. A good jazz band blended all of these ingredients with a little European classical music and a peppery seasoning of ragtime. A saucy layer of the blues was added for good measure. This African, European, ragtime, and blues mixture

14

swirled together and boiled over, like a rice pot, into some steaming, swinging jazz!

Louis loved the new jazz music. He borrowed ten dollars from a friend and purchased a secondhand cornet. It was all bent and had holes in it, but at least Louis had a horn to practice on. Black Benny Williams, the drummer, often listened to Louis when he played at the honky-tonks. One day, he took Louis to a picnic. Kid Ory, King Oliver, and their band were playing. Black Benny demanded that they let Louis play, and they did. Louis was so happy that his cornet seemed to sing.

As the years passed, more musicians started to pay attention to Louis. He often won musical dueling contests when he played against older cornet players. During a dueling contest, each musician played a solo. The notes would soar higher and

higher until one player was declared the winner. Everyone listened as Louis wailed out pure, clean high notes on his cornet. As he grew older, the other musicians began to call Louis "Satchelmouth" because of his large toothy smile. Soon, everyone was calling Louis "Satchmo" for short.

King Oliver was especially kind to Louis. He gave him another cornet, along with tips to improve his playing. King Oliver began to let Louis fill in for him while he rested between songs. Whenever King Oliver had too many musical engagements, he sent Louis to replace him.

Louis found a job driving a coal cart during the day. But at night, Louis was a first-class jazz musician. Man, oh, man!

5 MOVING TO CHICAGO

Around 1917, when Louis was sixteen, many of the jazz musicians in New Orleans started to move up North and out West. Jazz music began to spread out across the United States. Jazz bands were in big demand in Chicago, New York, and Los Angeles.

King Oliver decided to leave New Orleans and start his own band. He moved to Chicago and formed the Creole Jazz Band. There, every night at the Lincoln Gardens Café, the band played a spicy version of New Orleans jazz.

Kid Ory needed a good cornetist to replace King Oliver in his band. King Oliver recommended Louis. Louis was proud to be chosen, though he was sorry to see his old friend leave.

Louis loved playing in Kid Ory's band, but the work was not very steady. One day, Fate Marable, a bandleader on the riverboat S.S. *Sydney*, offered Louis a job. Louis sailed up and down the Mississippi River, playing for the parties and

17

dances that were held on board the riverboat. Every night the boat would dock at a small town or at one of the larger cities near the riverbank. Mr. Marable would play a rousing number on the calliope, a huge steam organ. Then the band would play for the crowds that gathered around the riverbank. Louis enjoyed traveling and playing on the *Sydney*. When there was time, the other band members taught Louis how to read music. Soon Louis was writing his own compositions. His first song was titled "I Wish I Could Shimmy Like My Sister Kate." It was the first of many songs that Louis would write.

Louis decided to join the Knights of Pythias, a social club. He often played for the club's street parades, picnics, parties, and funerals in New Orleans.

One day, after Louis had finished playing in a parade, someone handed him a telegram. It was from King Oliver. He wanted Louis to come to Chicago to play in his band. A chance to play with the King! Hurrah!

As soon as he could, Louis packed a bag, kissed his mother and Mama Lucy good-bye, and was on his way to Chicago. All the neighbors came to see him off. They shouted advice to Louis as he boarded the train with his small suitcase and a fish sandwich. Finally he was going to Chicago, the big time!

Louis got off the train at Illinois Central Station in Chicago at 11:30 P.M. No one was there at the dark, deserted station to meet him. King Oliver and his band were already on stage. Louis quickly took a cab to the Lincoln Gardens Café.

The Lincoln Gardens Café was one of the most beautiful places Louis had ever seen. A revolving cut-glass ball sprinkled slivers of light all over the balconied ballroom. A laughing crowd of well-dressed black men and women swayed to the music of King Oliver's band. Oh that wonderful music! King Oliver and the band were playing so fine, in $\frac{4}{4}$ time with a *boom-chicka-boom, boom-chicka* beat that moved everyone's feet. The drummer's riffs kept pace with Louis's heartbeat. The closer Louis got to the bandstand, the better the

19

band sounded. The saxophone screamed with joy, and the clarinet laughed up the scale and back down again. The fiery tones that King Oliver blew seemed to burn a hole in the smoky air. The more Louis listened, the sadder he felt. He would never be able to play that well.

The band members spotted Louis out in the crowd. "Here he is! Here he is!" they shouted. King Oliver jumped down from the bandstand and shook Louis's hand. "Have a seat, son, we're going to do our show," he said with a smile. "You might as well stick around and see what's happening. You start to work tomorrow night!"

"Yes sir!" said Louis happily.[3]

And from that time in 1922 onward, whether playing before audiences of kings, queens, or common people, Louis "Satchmo" Armstrong felt at home whenever he performed on the stage. After receiving an offer in 1924 to play with Fletcher Henderson and his orchestra, Louis left King

Louis (third from right) with King Oliver's Creole Jazz Band, 1923.

Oliver's band and headed for New York. This was Louis's first chance to travel as a musician.

The Henderson Orchestra toured all of the New England states and then took time off for a little swimming. "One of my favorite hobbies," Louis often said, "outside of typing!" Louis became famous for the long typewritten letters he sent to his friends.

One thing that Louis didn't like about working with Fletcher Henderson was that Henderson wouldn't let him sing. Louis began playing and recording with a variety of performers, including soprano saxophonist and clarinetist Sidney Bechet and the famous blues singers Ma Rainey, Billie Holiday, and Bessie Smith. Louis spent many hours in the recording studio singing and playing his music. After fourteen months and more than forty records, he left the orchestra and went back to Chicago.

6 THE AMBASSADOR OF JAZZ AND GOODWILL

Louis began forming his own bands. His first band was the Hot Five. Later, he formed the Hot Seven and then the All Stars. He also traded his cornet for the richer-sounding trumpet. In 1925, Louis became a lead performer on OKeh Records. He began to sing and make records with his bands. One day, while Louis was recording the song "Heebie Jeebies," the music slipped off the stand. Louis didn't want to stop the tape. He started to sing nonsense words "skeet scat scoot dut, a dut dut dat, oops pa dat do, oh yeahhh"—until someone handed him the music. This new style was called "scat" singing and became very popular. The audiences loved Louis's scat singing and his gravelly voice. Some singers even tried to catch a cold so that their voices would sound like his. Louis made some of the best-selling records in 1925 and 1926. His recordings of "Muskrat Ramble," "Cornet Chop

Suey," "Struttin' with Some Barbecue," and "West End Blues" sold thousands of copies.

Louis loved to perform. He played his music for audiences around the world. Louis's solos introduced a new kind of jazz to music lovers everywhere. Individual solos showcased the talents of every band member. Each musician could experiment freely with a song. Then, as easily as fingers slip into a glove, the band would swing back into one solid harmony. No one else could play those swinging, ringing, crystal clear, sky-high notes during a red-hot jazz solo like Satchmo!

Louis Armstrong became an ambassador of jazz and goodwill. He appeared in more than twenty-eight movies and was the first African-American performer to have his own radio show. In 1956, he visited West Africa and played for more than one hundred thousand people. His recordings of "When the Saints Go Marching In," "Mack the Knife," "What a Wonderful World," and his theme song, "Sleepytime Down South," made him one of the most popular jazz performers in modern times. Even though he was rich and successful, Louis never forgot those who were poor. He was known for his generosity, and he gave away thousands of dollars during his career.

Louis always spoke out when he felt something was wrong. In 1957, he was asked to tour Russia as a representative of the United States. During this time, black Americans in the South were

Louis Armstrong, 1930

*Louis on a European
tour, 1931*

Louis, top left, posing with his co-stars in the motion picture
New Orleans

By 1947, when he appeared in the movie New Orleans with Billie Holiday, Louis had become a star.

Louis meeting some of his fans in Tokyo, Japan, 1954

When he visited West Africa in 1957, Louis gave special attention to the children.

Louis in 1955

barred from entering schools attended by white students. They were also forced to use separate public bathrooms and water fountains. A black person could not sit in the front of a bus, try on clothing in a store owned by white people, or eat in the same restaurants as whites. Most jobs, restaurants, hotels, and recreational places were closed to black people.

Louis decided not to travel to Russia because of the unfair way blacks were treated in America. He also refused to play in any hotel where he couldn't stay as a guest because of his race.

"It's getting almost so bad," said Louis, "that a colored man hasn't got any country. If the people over there [in Russia] ask me what's wrong with my country, what am I supposed to say?"[4]

When his remarks were printed in the newspapers, many people were angry. Several of Louis's concerts were canceled. Some performers refused to appear on the same television shows when Louis was a guest. Louis was hurt by the angry newspaper articles written about him. But despite all the bad things that happened during this time, Louis insisted that he still had "a right to blow my top over injustice."[5]

7 BLOWING THAT HORN

In 1959, Louis had a heart attack. Although his health remained a problem for the rest of his life, Louis continued to record and perform. He made the most popular record of his career in 1963. *Hello, Dolly!* was a new Broadway musical, and Louis was asked to record the title song. The record was a best-selling hit for twenty-two weeks in 1964. Louis became more popular than ever. He also appeared in the movie *Hello, Dolly!* with the singer and actress Barbra Streisand.

Louis Armstrong married four times, but he never had any children. His fourth wife, Lucille Armstrong, had bought a wonderful home in Corona, Queens, in New York City. The neighborhood was full of children. Whenever Louis came back from a trip, they would help him carry his bags into the house. He watched his little friends grow up, marry, and have children of their own.

They always returned to visit Satchmo. He loved them and they loved him.

In June 1970, Louis had an early celebration for his seventieth birthday at the Newport Jazz Festival. Sixty-seven thousand fans stood cheering in the rain after his performance.

Ten months later, in April 1971, Louis was in very poor health. He could barely breathe and was having kidney problems. His doctor insisted that he go to the hospital, but Louis refused. He had an engagement at the Empire Room of the Waldorf-Astoria Hotel in New York City.

"Louie," said Dr. Zucker, "you could drop dead while you're performing."

"Doc," Louis said, "that's all right, I don't care. Doc, you don't understand. My whole life, my whole soul, my whole spirit is to blooow that hooorn."[6]

When the performance ended, Louis agreed to check into Beth Israel Hospital. After a few weeks in the hospital, Louis returned to the home he loved so much in Corona. On July 6, 1971, Louis "Satchmo" Armstrong, one of the greatest jazz artists in the world, died of kidney failure.

Newspapers and magazines around the world wrote about Louis and his contribution to music. His funeral was attended by thousands and was covered on national television.

Louis Armstrong's records, movies, and personal appearances introduced jazz music to thousands of

In 1963, Louis recorded the title song of a new Broadway musical, Hello, Dolly!

In 1970, Louis celebrated his seventieth birthday at the Newport Jazz Festival in Rhode Island. Thousands of fans and colleagues attended.

people. He justly deserves much of the credit for popularizing the stirring solos, sweet harmonies, and complex melodies that are part of black America's musical gift to the world. Louis "Satchmo" Armstrong taught the world to swing!

CHRONOLOGY

1901 Louis is born in New Orleans, Louisiana, on August 4

1913 Sent to the Colored Waifs' Home; learns to play the cornet

1914 Released from the Home; begins playing his cornet with older musicians around New Orleans

1917 Joe "King" Oliver leaves Kid Ory's Orchestra; Louis replaces him

1918 Marries Daisy Parker

1922 Leaves New Orleans for Chicago; begins playing with King Oliver's Creole Jazz Band

1924 Marries Lillian Hardin; joins Fletcher Henderson's Orchestra in New York City

1925 Makes his first records for the OKeh label with his band, the Hot Five

1929 *Hot Chocolates* opens on Broadway with Louis in starring role

1938 Marries Alpha Smith

1942 Marries Lucille Wilson; moves to Corona, Queens, New York

1956 Tours Africa as goodwill ambassador for the State Department

1957 Speaks out against racism in America; refuses to tour Russia as goodwill ambassador for the State Department

1959 Suffers a heart attack

1964 "Hello, Dolly!" becomes best-selling record in America

1971 Dies of kidney failure on July 6

ENDNOTES

1. Armstrong, Louis. *Satchmo: My Life in New Orleans* (New York: Prentice-Hall, 1954), p. 30.
2. Ibid., p. 35.
3. Ibid., p. 185
4. Giddens, Gary. *Satchmo* (New York: Bantam Doubleday Dell Publishing Group, Inc., 1988), p. 163
5. Ibid.
6. Collier, James Lincoln. *Louis Armstrong: An American Genius* (New York: Oxford University Press, 1983), p. 331.

FURTHER READING
FOR CHILDREN

Collier, James Lincoln. *Louis Armstrong: An American Success Story.* New York: Macmillan, 1985

Eaton, Jeanette. *Trumpeter's Tale: The Story of Young Louis Armstrong.* New York: William Morrow, 1955.

Haskins, James. *The Creoles of Color of New Orleans.* New York: Thomas Y. Crowell, 1975.

Iverson, Genie. *Louis Armstrong.* New York: Thomas Y. Crowell, 1976.

Millender, Dharathula H. *Louis Armstrong: Young Music Maker.* New York: Bobbs-Merrill Co., 1972.

Tanenhaus, Sam. *Louis Armstrong.* New York: Chelsea House, 1988.

BIBLIOGRAPHY

Armstrong, Louis. *Satchmo: My Life in New Orleans*. New York: Prentice-Hall, 1954.

Collier, James Lincoln. *Louis Armstrong: An American Genius*. New York: Oxford University Press, 1983.

————. *The Making of Jazz: A Comprehensive History*. Boston: Houghton Mifflin, 1978.

Feather, Leonard G. *From Satchmo to Miles*. New York: Stein and Day, 1972.

Giddens, Gary. *Satchmo*. New York: Bantam Doubleday Dell Publishing Group, Inc., 1988.

Morgenstern, Dan. *Jazz People*. New York: Harry N. Abrams, 1976.

INDEX

Page numbers in *italics* refer to photographs.